I Can Brush My Teeth

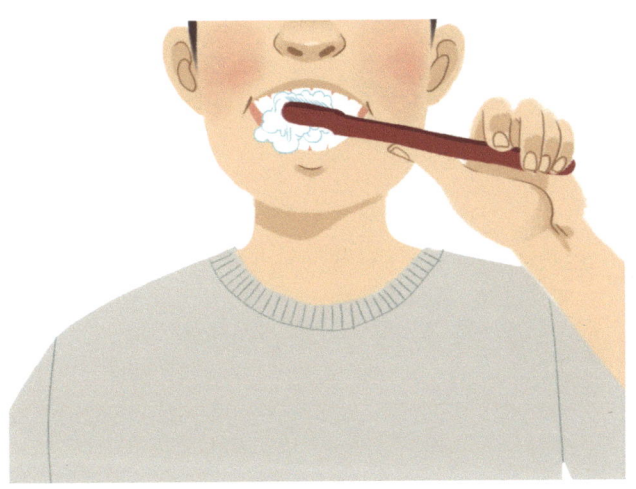

Written by Chemise Taylor

Illustrated by Alexis B. Taylor

Copyright © 2019 by My Skills Books

Published by My Skills Books

All rights reserved. No part of this publication may be reproduced, distributed, or transmitted in any form or by any means, including photocopying, recording, or other electronic or mechanical methods, without the prior written permission of the publisher, except in the case of brief quotations embodied in critical reviews and certain other noncommercial uses permitted by copyright law.

First Printing, 2019.

ISBN: 978-1-951573-05-8

www.myskillsbooks.com

It's time to start the day and brush my teeth.

I get my toothbrush and toothpaste.

I turn on the sink faucet.

I wet the toothbrush bristles with water.

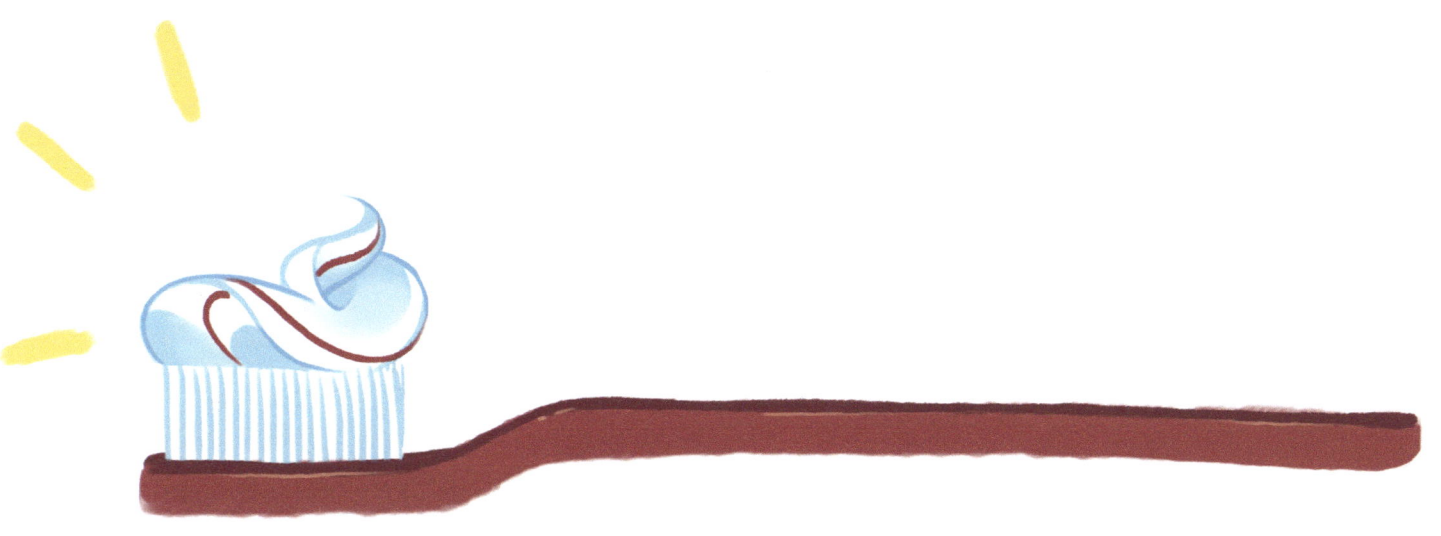

I squeeze toothpaste onto the toothbrush.

I brush the front of my teeth.

I brush my top, left teeth.

I brush my bottom, left teeth.

I brush my top, right teeth.

I brush my bottom, right teeth.

I rinse off my toothbrush.

I get a cup of water and rinse my mouth.

Then, I spit the water in the sink.

Finally, I turn off the sink faucet.

All done! Now my teeth are clean.

Book Details

Story Word Count: 110

Primary Reading Grade Level(s): Preschool, Kindergarten, First Grade

Key Words: Brush, Teeth, Toothbrush, Toothpaste, Sink, Water, Tongue, Spit

Comprehension Check
- What was the story about?
- What did he put on his toothbrush?
- What did he rinse his mouth with?

Reading Award

This certificate goes to:

_____

for reading "I Can Brush My Teeth"

Good Job!

More books, apps and resources at myskillsbooks.com

www.ingramcontent.com/pod-product-compliance
Lightning Source LLC
Chambersburg PA
CBHW042108090526
44591CB00004B/47